Ultimate FACTIVITY Collection

BUGS

Create your own book about the world of creepy crawlies

DK | Penguin Random House

Project Editor James Mitchem
Senior Designers Clare Shedden, Sadie Thomas
Designer Samantha Richiardi
Design Assistance Charlotte Bull, Stefan Georgiou
Consultant David Burnie
Jacket Art Editor Kathryn Wilding
Illustrators Chris Howker, Jake McDonald

Producer Rebecca Fallowfield
Senior Producer Ché Creasey
Creative Technical Support Sonia Charbonnier
Managing Editor Penny Smith
Senior Managing Art Editor Marianne Markham
Publisher Mary Ling
Creative Director Jane Bull

First published in Great Britain in 2015 by
Dorling Kindersley Limited
One Embassy Gardens, 8 Viaduct Gardens,
London, SW11 7BW

A CIP catalogue record for this book
is available from the British Library.
ISBN: 978-0-2411-8080-8

Printed and bound in China

For the curious
www.dk.com

All about arthropods

When people say "bugs" or "creepy-crawlies" they're usually thinking about insects. But insects are actually just one type of creature in a much larger group called arthropods.

Page _____

Page _____

Page _____

Page _____

Page _____

Page _____

FIND these pictures on pages 4–17 and write the page numbers in the boxes.

Don't forget to put your stickers in first.

What is an arthropod?

Is that beetle an arthropod?

Arthropods are the biggest group of animals on Earth, and they're also the most varied. However, there are **three things** that all arthropods have in common.

STICK the stickers in place to reveal the arthropod.

1 Arthropods have **exoskeletons**. Their bodies are hard on the outside and soft on the inside.

Exoskeletons are a bit like a suit of armour.

2 All arthropods have **segmented bodies**. Which means their bodies are split into two or more parts.

3 Arthropods have six or more **jointed legs.** In fact, the word arthropod means "jointed foot".

TRUE OR FALSE?

Many species of arthropod are so tiny that they're actually too small to see.

Tiger Beetle

All insects are arthropods, but not all arthropods are insects!

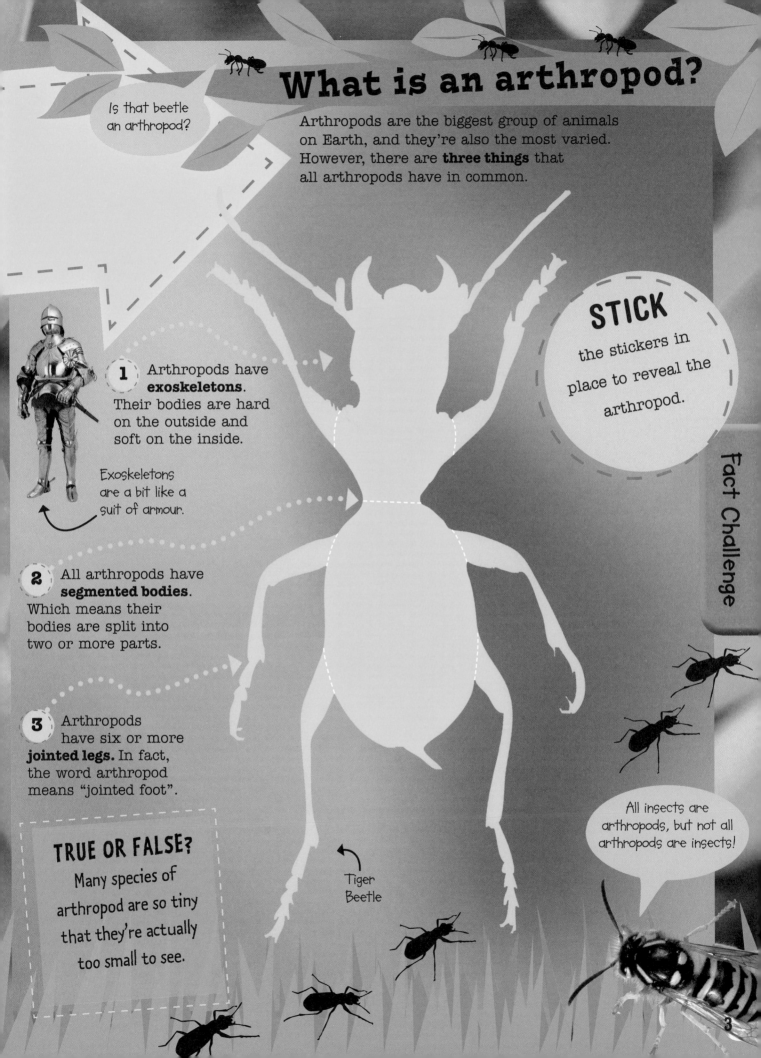

3

What do I look like?

DRAW each creature using the clues as a guide. Then stick in the real versions.

There are around a million different arthropod species, and they come in a variety of shapes and sizes. Do you think you can draw them accurately?

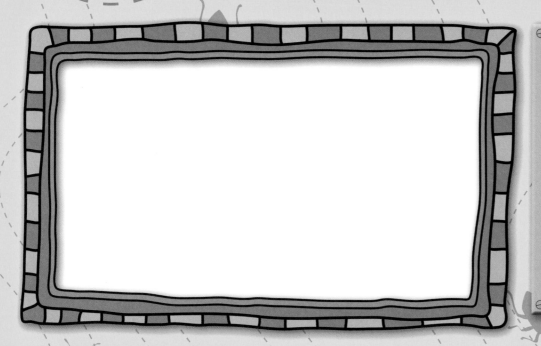

TIGER CENTIPEDE
- Its long body is made up of 20 little segments.
- Each segment alternates between orange and black.
- It has two long antennae on its head.
- It has around 20 pairs of legs!

RED KNEED TARANTULA
- Has eight thick legs.
- Its body and legs are covered in small hairs.
- All of its knees are an orangey red colour.
- Has a thick body split into two parts.

MONARCH BUTTERFLY
- Its body is long and slender.
- Has two pairs of wings.
- Its wings are bright orange with black lines and little white spots around the edges.
- Has two thin antennae on its head.

AMERICAN LOBSTER
- Is a bluey green colour.
- Its body is covered in a hard shell.
- Has 10 legs, including its claws.
- Its front two claws are much thicker and bigger.
- One claw is often bigger than the other.

Insects

Stick insects

Cockroaches

Termites

Mantises

Grasshoppers

Earwigs

Dragonflies

Millipedes

Myriapods

Centipedes

Harvestmen

Scorpions

Spiders

Arachnids

These are just the main types of arthropod you will meet.

Arthropod families

People often think that all "creepy-crawlies" are insects, but that's not true. Insects are just one group of creature in a much larger group called arthropods.

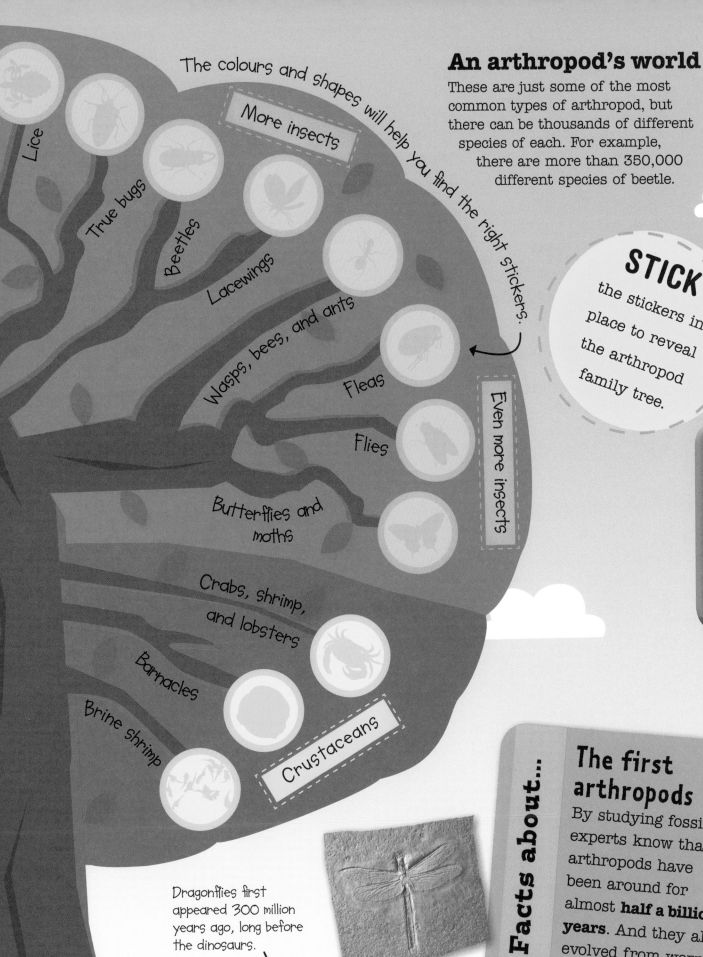

An arthropod's world

These are just some of the most common types of arthropod, but there can be thousands of different species of each. For example, there are more than 350,000 different species of beetle.

The colours and shapes will help you find the right stickers.

Lice

True bugs

Beetles

Lacewings

More insects

Wasps, bees, and ants

Fleas

Flies

Even more insects

Butterflies and moths

Crabs, shrimp, and lobsters

Barnacles

Brine shrimp

Crustaceans

STICK the stickers in place to reveal the arthropod family tree.

Fact Challenge

Dragonflies first appeared 300 million years ago, long before the dinosaurs.

Facts about...

The first arthropods

By studying fossils, experts know that arthropods have been around for almost **half a billion years**. And they all evolved from worms!

Count my legs

It can be hard to tell if a creature is an insect or another type of arthropod. There are a few ways to tell them apart, but one of the easiest ways is to look at their legs.

COUNT
how many legs each creature has and write which type each one is.

Spider pedipalps (which are for feeling or holding) aren't legs.

A spider has ____ legs and is an

_____

A wasp has ____ legs and is an

_____

6 **Insect:** If a creature has 6 legs it's probably an insect. Most of them have a body that is divided into three sections: a head, a thorax (chest), and an abdomen (belly).

8 **Arachnid:** Most people know spiders and scorpions, but ticks and mites are arachnids too. They all have 8 legs, and none has wings.

10 **Crustacean:** While some crustaceans live on land, most of them live in water. They usually have 10 legs but some can have more.

30+ **Myriapoda:** If a creature has lots of legs, it's probably a centipede or millipede. These have long bodies made up of lots of segments.

A weevil has ____ legs and is an ____

A ladybird has ____ legs and is an ____

Pedipalps look like legs, but they're not.

A crab has ____ legs and is a ____

These claws count as legs.

A scorpion has ____ legs and is an ____

A millipede has lots of ____ legs and is a ____
Myriapoda

Millipede means "a thousand feet", but most actually have a few hundred.

Earth's most successful creatures

TEST yourself to see how much you know about arthropods.

It might seem like humans rule the world, but arthropods have been around for a lot longer, and there are many more of them than any other type of creature on Earth.

Don't worry if you don't know the answers. You will soon!

1
There are 7,000,000,000 (7 billion) humans on Earth. But how many insects are there to every human?

Hint: it's a very big number!

A 1,000,000 (1 million) ☐

B 15,000,000 (15 million) ☐

C 200,000,000 (200 million) ☐

2
The largest group of arthropods are insects. How many estimated species of insect are there?

Hint: there are more than 350,000 species of beetle.

A 90,000 (90 thousand) ☐

B 900,000 (900 thousand) ☐

C 90,000,000 (90 million) ☐

3 What percentage of all animals on Earth are arthropods?

Hint: there are quite a lot more of us than any other creature.

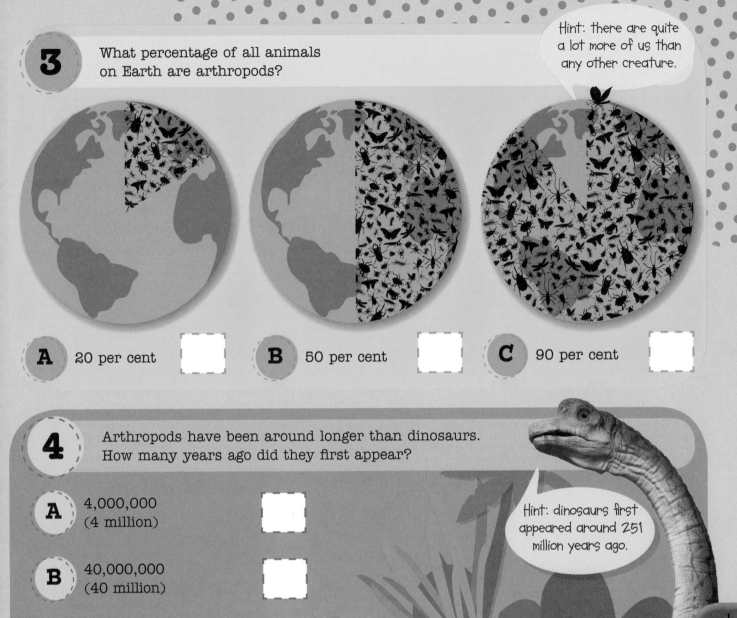

A 20 per cent

B 50 per cent

C 90 per cent

4 Arthropods have been around longer than dinosaurs. How many years ago did they first appear?

A 4,000,000 (4 million)

B 40,000,000 (40 million)

C 400,000,000 (400 million)

Hint: dinosaurs first appeared around 251 million years ago.

5 1 sqm (10 sqft) of forest floor can contain up to how many arthropods?

Hint: the forest floor is absolutely packed with life.

A 50,000 (50 thousand)

B 500,000 (500 thousand)

C 1,500,000 (1 and half million)

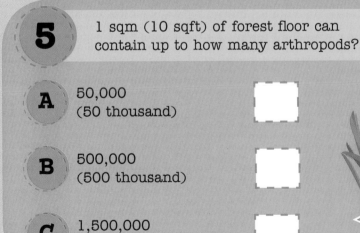

Butterfly

READ about butterflies and moths, and stick stickers into the correct circles.

The Queen Alexandra's birdwing is the largest butterfly in the world.

? Butterflies can only fly when their bodies are warm enough. So they only **fly at day** or dusk – not night.

? Most butterflies have long, **thin antennae** with rounded tips at the end.

? Almost all butterflies have thin and **smooth bodies**.

? When resting, most butterflies position their wings so that they're **upright** and together.

? A butterfly's **chrysalis** has a hard shell and usually hangs from a leaf.

Butterflies

These pretty insects are best-known for their bright colours and symmetrical wing patterns. Did you know they're related to moths?

Butterflies and moths both belong to the same group of insects, and in many ways they're very similar. However, there are a few simple ways to tell them apart.

or Moth?

With a wingspan of up to 30cm (12in) the Atlas Moth is the biggest in the world.

Moths

Most people probably think of moths as the dull looking creatures that ruin our clothes, but they can also come in lots of beautiful colours as well.

Some moths fly during the day, but most **fly by night**. They vibrate their flight muscles to warm up.

?

Moth's **antennae** are more like brushes. They use them to sense their way at night.

?

Moth's **bodies** are thicker than butterflies, and covered with fuzz to keep them warm.

?

A moth will usually rest with its **wings open** and flat.

?

Instead of a chrysalis, most moths spin a **cocoon** on or under the ground.

?

A magnified view of a butterfly wing.

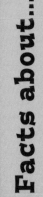

Facts about...

Scaly wings

Butterfly and moth wings look soft, but they are made of lots of hard **chitin** scales – a material very similar to keratin, which is what our fingernails are made of.

Lots of legs

Millipedes and centipedes belong to a group of arthropods called Myriapods. They may look like insects at first, but there's one key difference – the number of legs they have!

I have two pairs of legs on each segment. Can you draw the rest?

Millipedes

The Latin word "mil' means thousand, but most millipedes have around 60 legs (though some have as many as 750).

Centipedes

A lot of people think all centipedes have 100 legs, but the number actually ranges from about 20 to 300.

 Feeds on plants.

Will sink in water.

Feeds on small animals.

Will float in water.

Facts about...

Fossils

Myriapoda are one of the **oldest types** of arthropod – a centipede fossil has been found that dates back almost 430 million years.

Centipedes can be poisonous.

Poisonous centipedes can inject their prey with a paralyzing venom.

DRAW

the rest of the legs on the millipede and centipede, then colour them in.

Pill millipedes look like woodlice, but they have more legs.

Moves very slowly.	Rolls into a coil when attacked.	Has four legs on each body segment.	Usually have round bodies.
Moves very quickly.	Runs away if attacked.	Has one pair of legs on each body segment.	Usually have flat bodies.

I have a pair of legs on each segment. Can you draw the rest?

The word myriapoda means "many legs".

Under the sea

Crabs can walk on land, but almost all crustaceans live in water. Woodlice are one of the few species that live on land.

STICK crustaceans into the scene, then draw one of your own.

Goose barnacles

I'm a hermit crab. As I grow I need to find new shells to live in.

Barnacles

DRAW and **COLOUR** your own crustacean scene. Fill it with crabs, lobsters, shrimp, and more!

Working with bugs

There are far more arthropods on Earth than any other type of animal, so there are lots of different jobs that involve studying, harvesting, and managing them.

Don't forget to put your stickers in first.

Page _____

Page _____

FIND

these pictures on pages 20–33 and write the page numbers in the boxes.

Page _____

Page _____

Page _____

Page _____

What do I do?

Pest exterminator   Conservationist   Entomologist

Forensic entomologist   Beekeeper

MATCH

each job to the description and add stickers in each of the outlines.

1 I help to **manage colonies of bees** so that I can gather their delicious honey.

I am a _____

2 I'm called to crime scenes to **study** flies and maggots for important clues.

I am a _____

3 I work to conserve and protect wildlife and the environment.

I am a _____

4 I help to get rid of **annoying pests** that cause all sorts of problems for people.

I am a _____

5 It's my job to **study** insect species to learn more about them.

I am an _____

Adult and baby

Insects and other arthropods don't grow up in the same way as most other creatures do. Instead of just getting bigger they can completely change size, colour, and shape.

Facts about...

Life cycles
Most insects go through several different changes before becoming adults, but almost all of them **hatch from eggs** before becoming larvae.

The **yellow swallowtail caterpillar** has a stripy body with orange spots.

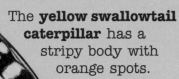

Ladybird larvae have long thin bodies with several small coloured spots.

The larvae of **bluebottle flies** are maggots that feed on decaying flesh and rubbish.

Mayfly babies (nymphs) are brown in colour and are good swimmers.

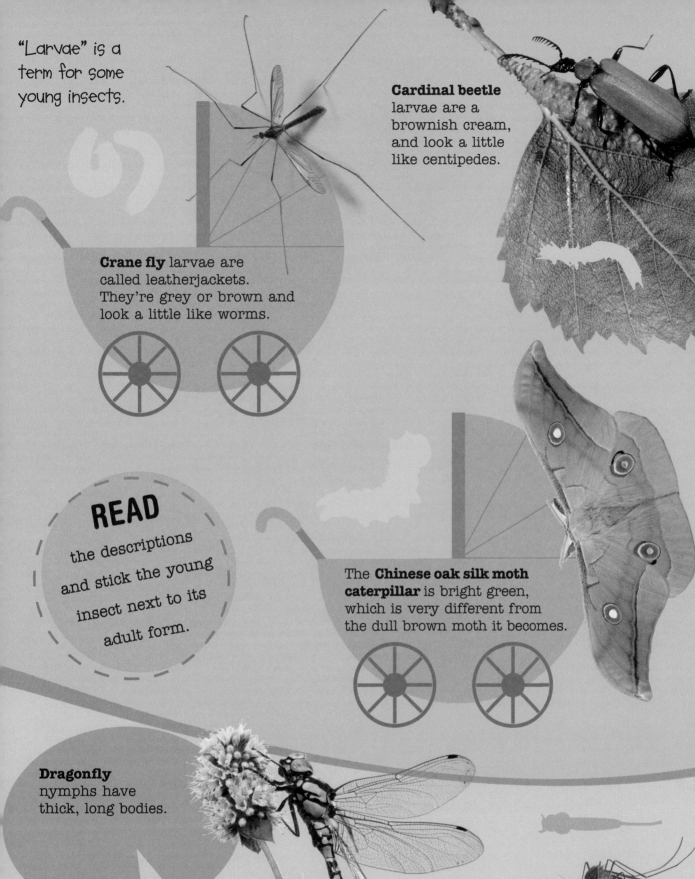

"Larvae" is a term for some young insects.

Cardinal beetle larvae are a brownish cream, and look a little like centipedes.

Crane fly larvae are called leatherjackets. They're grey or brown and look a little like worms.

READ

the descriptions and stick the young insect next to its adult form.

The **Chinese oak silk moth caterpillar** is bright green, which is very different from the dull brown moth it becomes.

Dragonfly nymphs have thick, long bodies.

The larvae of **mosquitos** must live in water for several weeks. Their bodies are long and slim.

Insect superpowers

Insects may be small, but that doesn't mean they're not special. Because of the way the laws of physics work on tiny things, it can seem like they have superpowers.

I can walk up walls with ease! Can you?

TICK

whether you think each statement is true or false.

1

If the cat flea was the size of a human it would be able to jump as high as Mt Everest.

TRUE ○ FALSE ○

850 times a human's weight would be as much as a tank!

2

The rhinoceros beetle can lift 850 times its own body weight.

TRUE ○ FALSE ○

Forces

Insects don't really have superpowers, it just seems like they do because **forces that involve weight** such as jumping and lifting are much easier at such tiny sizes.

3

Some species of fly are totally invisible, and can only be seen with special glasses.

TRUE ○ ○ FALSE

4

Certain ants are so strong they can drag objects 1,500 times as heavy as them.

TRUE ○ ○ FALSE

5

Moths are so light, they can fly as fast as a jumbo jet.

TRUE ○ ○ FALSE

6

Pond skaters can walk on water without ever sinking.

TRUE ○ ○ FALSE

Danger!

Here are several ways that arthropods can cause harm.

CONNECT the dots to reveal the rest of the picture, then colour it in.

Spiky surprise

The **postman caterpillar** has two means of defence. Not only is it poisonous, but its soft body is covered in sharp protective spikes.

Tail barb

Scorpions, like the **desert scorpion**, have barbed tails which can be used to paralyze or sometimes kill their enemies.

Deadly bite

Not all spiders have a deadly bite, but the **black widow's** is so venomous it can kill small animals and even sometimes people.

A nasty sting

Like bees, **wasps** use their stingers to hurt their enemies. Unlike bees though, wasps can sting repeatedly and survive.

They may be small, but that doesn't mean they're harmless. Many arthropods have developed deadly ways of attacking prey or fighting back against predators.

Chemical spray

The bombardier beetle stores the chemicals inside **two separate parts** of its body. When attacked, it mixes them, causing them to react and explode.

Draw and Learn

A surprising spray

The bombardier beetle has an unusual way of defending itself. It fends off predators by spraying boiling chemicals at them. Smaller predators can be blinded or even killed by it.

Aphids eat their way through a lot of plants and crops, so are the enemies of gardeners and farmers.

Fleas can infest dogs, cats, and humans. They suck blood for food and it causes intense itching and pain.

Helpful or harmful?

STICK a helpful, harmful, or both stickers in place depending on what you think.

Most insects are harmless to humans, and play a vital part in nature by providing food for other creatures and recycling waste, but others are pests that cause big problems.

Facts about...

The food chain

Every insect, no matter how tiny or insignificant it might seem, has an effect on the food chain. **So all insects are important**, even if they're also harmful.

Fruit flies create unsanitary conditions, but scientists have studied and used them in genetics experiments.

Maggots feed on dead flesh and doctors have used them to clean wounds, but they breed in large numbers and can cause infestations.

Bees pollinate plants, which helps us to grow food, but their sting can be deadly to people with allergies.

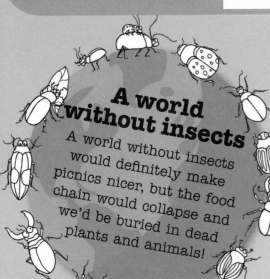

A world without insects

A world without insects would definitely make picnics nicer, but the food chain would collapse and we'd be buried in dead plants and animals!

Maggots are the larvae of flies.

Many insects are helpful because they control other insect populations.

Termites eat wood, which causes problems in houses and other buildings. But they also help to recycle dead and decaying trees.

Dung beetles feed on decaying material and the dung of other creatures. This cleans the waste and keeps the soil healthy.

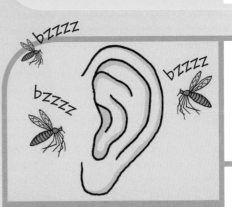

bzzzz

bzzzz

bzzzz

Female **mosquitos** carry and spread many deadly diseases such as malaria and dengue fever.

Fact Challenge

Insects and other arthropods have adapted to be able to blend into their surroundings and stay hidden. They do this for two reasons: to hide from predators, or to surprise their prey.

The **forest leaf grasshopper** looks so much like a leaf that it's almost impossible to tell the difference even when you know it's there!

They may look like ordinary thorns on a branch, but they're actually **thorn bugs** (or treehoppers) If you look closely you can see their legs.

It's more common in moths, but butterflies such as the **cracker butterfly** can look like the bark of a tree while perched.

The colour and markings of a **stick caterpillar** make it very difficult to tell it apart from a branch or twig. It's very hard for a predator to spot.

When **leaf insects** move their bodies rock back and forth. This makes them look just like a leaf being blown in the wind.

Is that a leaf?

What a good disguise!

Facts about...

Camouflage

Blending in like this is called camouflage. It's not just animals that do this. **Army uniforms** are made to be camouflaged so that soldiers are harder to spot.

STICK

the stickers in to reveal the hidden insect and finish the sticker puzzle.

Can you spot the hiding mantis?

This shield bug would be hard to spot among leaves.

A hidden threat

While most bugs blend in to protect themselves, others, such as mantises, do it to remain hidden so they can ambush prey.

29

Eating bugs

Arthropods are an important source of food. In fact, up to 80 per cent of the world's population eat them regularly.

STICK

insects, crustaceans, and arachnids on the dinner plate. Yum!

TRUE OR FALSE?
The word for humans eating insects is "entomophagy".

Facts about...

Insect meals

Not all arthropods are edible – lots of them are poisonous. It's thought that there are roughly **12,000** different species that are eaten by humans.

Dinner time

Crustaceans such as lobsters and crabs are arthropods that lots of people eat. Here are a few others you might not know about.

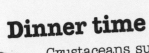

Menu

Prawns are cooked in a variety of ways all over the world.

Silkworm pupae are most popular in Japan, but are eaten across Asia.

Water bugs are usually deep fried and covered with salt.

Mealworms are eaten as healthy and crunchy snacks.

Scorpions are cooked on skewers in Thailand and China.

Crickets are a very nutritious snack that are usually toasted.

Let's fly

People like to call bugs creepy-crawlies, but a surprisingly large number of them can take to the air and soar through the sky!

FILL the sky with flying insects and then draw your own winged creature.

I have a set of hard wings that protect the ones I fly with. Can you see me flying?

DRAW and **COLOUR** your own flying insect. Think about how many wings you'd like it to have and if you'd like it to be brightly coloured.

The arthropod world

Insects and other arthropods experience and interact with the world in a very different way from us. Turn the pages to discover just how different they really are.

FIND these pictures on pages 36–49 and write the page numbers in the boxes.

Page _____

Page _____

Page _____

Page _____

Page _____

Page _____

Don't forget to put your stickers in first.

FOLLOW
the lines to match each description to its picture, then add the correct sticker.

Seeing together

Most arthropod's eyes are made up of lots of tiny lenses. Each of these lenses sends a different image to their brain. This is called **compound eyesight**.

Insects don't have eyelids.

The **stalk-eyed fly's** eyes are attached to the ends of long narrow stalks that are almost the same length as its body.

Most **spiders** have eight eyes but they don't have very good eyesight. Instead, they use their sense of touch to find their way around.

Dragonflies' eyes are bigger than the rest of their heads. They can spot prey in all directions while flying through the air.

When light is reflected from the shiny lenses in a **horsefly's** eye, it can create a very pretty rainbow pattern.

Praying mantises have binocular vision, which helps them to judge distances when striking. They're one of the few insects that can do this.

Most insects cannot see prey well unless it's moving around.

Fact Challenge

Bugs & co shopping

How may I help you?

FOLLOW the lines to discover what each arthropod gives us and write the number in the box.

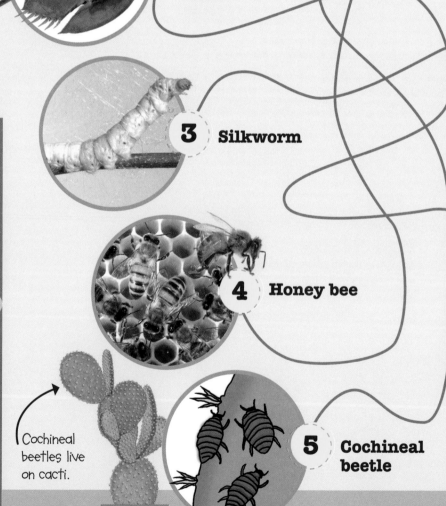

1 No-see-um

2 Horseshoe crab

3 Silkworm

4 Honey bee

5 Cochineal beetle

OPEN

Pollination

By far the most important thing that insects do for us is pollinating plants. Without them doing this we wouldn't be able to grow crops for food. Bats and birds pollinate as well, but not as much as insects.

Cochineal beetles live on cacti.

Arthropods do a lot of work for the planet, but they're also useful to humans in other ways. This includes scientific research or helping us create various products.

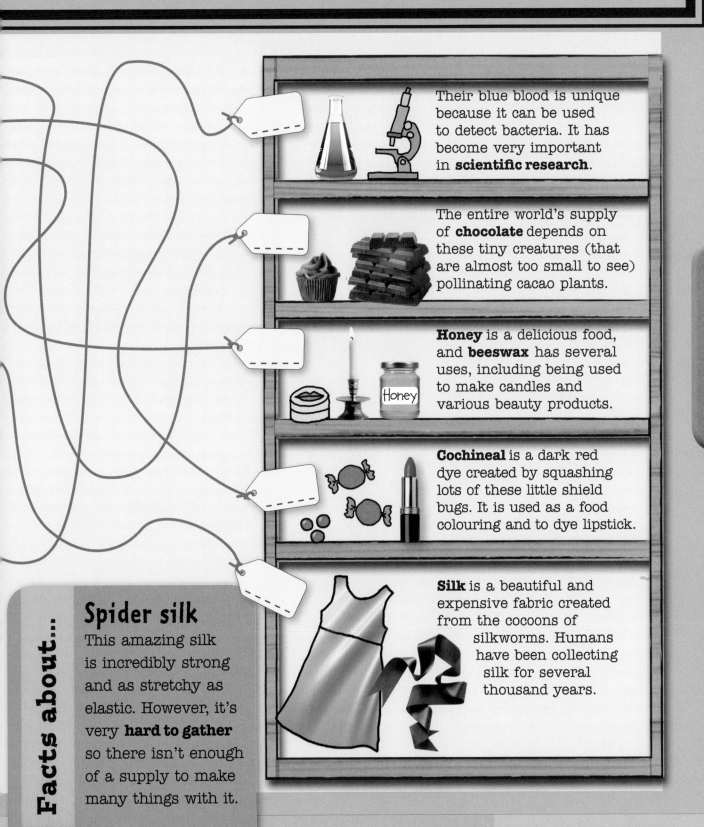

Their blue blood is unique because it can be used to detect bacteria. It has become very important in **scientific research**.

The entire world's supply of **chocolate** depends on these tiny creatures (that are almost too small to see) pollinating cacao plants.

Honey is a delicious food, and **beeswax** has several uses, including being used to make candles and various beauty products.

Honey

Cochineal is a dark red dye created by squashing lots of these little shield bugs. It is used as a food colouring and to dye lipstick.

Silk is a beautiful and expensive fabric created from the cocoons of silkworms. Humans have been collecting silk for several thousand years.

Fact Challenge

Facts about...

Spider silk

This amazing silk is incredibly strong and as stretchy as elastic. However, it's very **hard to gather** so there isn't enough of a supply to make many things with it.

Army of ants

Ants might look tiny and unimportant, but they're impressive insects that live in complex societies. In fact, they're some of the most successful species on Earth.

ANSWER whether you think each of the facts at the bottom are true or false.

Facts about...

Teamwork

Ant colonies can be home for up to **thousands** of ants, so cooperation is very important. Ants build together, work together, and they raise their young together.

Ant biology

There are more than 35,000 species of ant, and they vary in size from about 2mm (0.08in) to 2.5cm (1in) long. However, the body shape of most species is quite similar.

Stick the labels in the right places.

Antennae

?????

?????

?????

Head

Thorax

?????

?????

1

Ants have been around for almost 250 million years.

TRUE FALSE

2

Ants are closely related to wasps and bees.

TRUE FALSE

3

Fire ants all attack at the same time so they can cause more damage.

TRUE FALSE

38

Ants vs humans

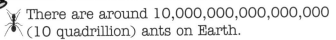 There are around 10,000,000,000,000,000 (10 quadrillion) ants on Earth.

There are around 7,000,000,000 (7 billion) humans on Earth.

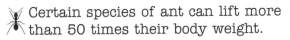 Certain species of ant can lift more than 50 times their body weight.

Most humans can't lift their own body weight.

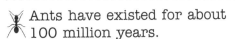 Ants have existed for about 100 million years.

Humans have existed for about 3 million years.

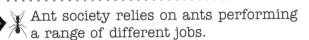 Ant society relies on ants performing a range of different jobs.

Human society does too.

Almost all the ants in a colony are female.

About half of humans are female.

While most ants look quite similar, different species have different traits. This ant has **large mandibles** to help it attack and defend.

4

A species of ant found in Japan can grow to be 1m (3ft) long.

TRUE FALSE

5

The only continent where ants aren't found is Antarctica.

TRUE FALSE

6

The bullet ant has the most painful bite or sting of any insect.

TRUE FALSE

Harvestmen look like spiders but can't spin webs. They also don't have fangs like spiders.

Scorpions use their powerful pincers (called pedipalps) to catch prey and then sting it with their deadly tail barb.

Many species of **spider**, such as the wasp spider, trap prey in their webs and inject them with a paralyzing venom.

STICK
the stickers into the frames to complete the arachnid pictures.

What's an arachnid?

I can hang in the air from one strand of my spider silk.

They may look like insects, but arachnids are totally different creatures. There are lots of types, but the one thing they have in common is that they all have 8 legs.

Not all spiders spin webs, but those that do create many different patterns.

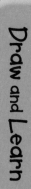

Whip scorpions use their six short legs to walk sideways while feeling for prey with their long front legs (whips).

Some **spiders** don't catch their prey using webs. Instead they lie in wait ready to ambush their victims.

Actual size of a redlegged earth mite.

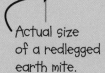

Mites and ticks are usually too small to see but they're everywhere. A person's bed might contain millions!

Facts about...

Spider silk

The webs that spiders spin are made of something called spider silk, which is five times **stronger than a piece of steel** that is the same thickness.

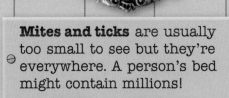

Beetle box

Of all the insect species in the world, a third of them are beetles. They're also some of Earth's most diverse creatures, and come in all different sizes, shapes, and colours.

TRUE OR FALSE?
There are an estimated 350,000 different species of beetle in the world.

MATCH the rest of the beetles to the outlines and stick them in the correct place.

The **hercules beetle** belongs to the rhinoceros beetle family, and can lift more than 850 times its own body weight.

The heaviest beetle in the world, the **goliath beetle** can weigh as much as 100g (3½oz) and grow to be 15cm (6in) long.

Famous for their antennae that can be longer than their bodies, there are more than 20,000 species of **longhorn beetle**.

The **stag beetle** is one of the best-known species of beetle in the world. Males have powerful jaws to fight its rivals.

Unlike most beetles, **click beetles** can move their heads and front pair of legs separately from the rest of the body.

Wings

Most beetles have two pairs of wings, one for flying, and **a second hardened pair** to protect the ones they fly with. These hard wings are called elytra.

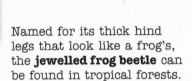

Named for its thick hind legs that look like a frog's, the **jewelled frog beetle** can be found in tropical forests.

The rare **precious metal scarab beetle**, which is usually gold or silver colour, can sometimes be found in parts of South America.

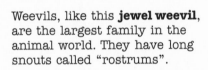

Male **giraffe weevils** have very long necks, which can be up to three times as long as the female's.

Weevils, like this **jewel weevil**, are the largest family in the animal world. They have long snouts called "rostrums".

The ancient Egyptians believed the **scarab beetle** symbolized the restoration of life. It can be seen in lots of ancient art.

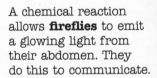

The **Namibian fog-basking darkling beetle** survives by collecting moisture from fog that rolls in from the coast.

The **violin beetle** has a flat body so it can fit between the layers of fungi that grow on the trees where it lives.

This **African jewel beetle** possibly gathers pollen on its back so predators can't see it while it sits on flowers.

A chemical reaction allows **fireflies** to emit a glowing light from their abdomen. They do this to communicate.

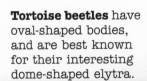

Sometimes called a June bug, the **green June beetle** has dull green wings and a shiny green underside.

The colourful **lily leaf beetle** feeds on lily plants, and is considered a pest by gardeners.

Most commonly red, **ladybirds** can also be yellow, orange, or black. The number of spots they have varies.

Tortoise beetles have oval-shaped bodies, and are best known for their interesting dome-shaped elytra.

Termite skyscraper

Termites are the master architects of the insect world. Their colonies can be absolutely huge, and even have a working air-conditioning system!

TRUE OR FALSE?

If termites were the size of humans their nests would be up to 600m (2000ft) tall.

DRAW

a route through the termite maze. Look out for dead ends!

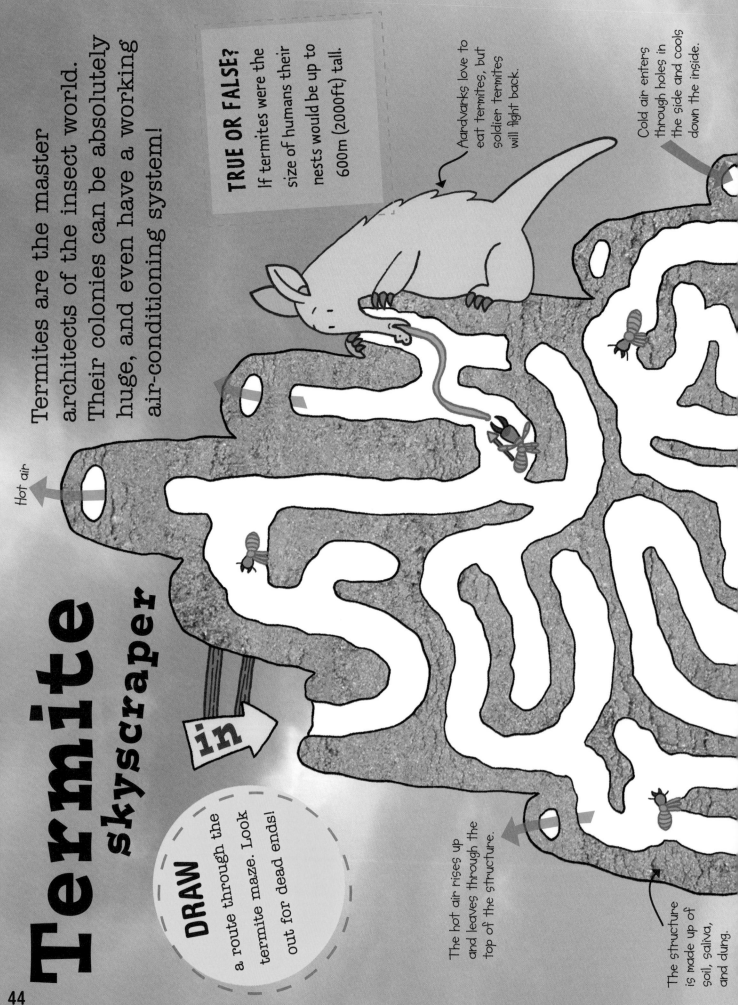

Hot air

in

Aardvarks love to eat termites, but soldier termites will fight back.

Cold air enters through holes in the side and cools down the inside.

The hot air rises up and leaves through the top of the structure.

The structure is made up of soil, saliva, and dung.

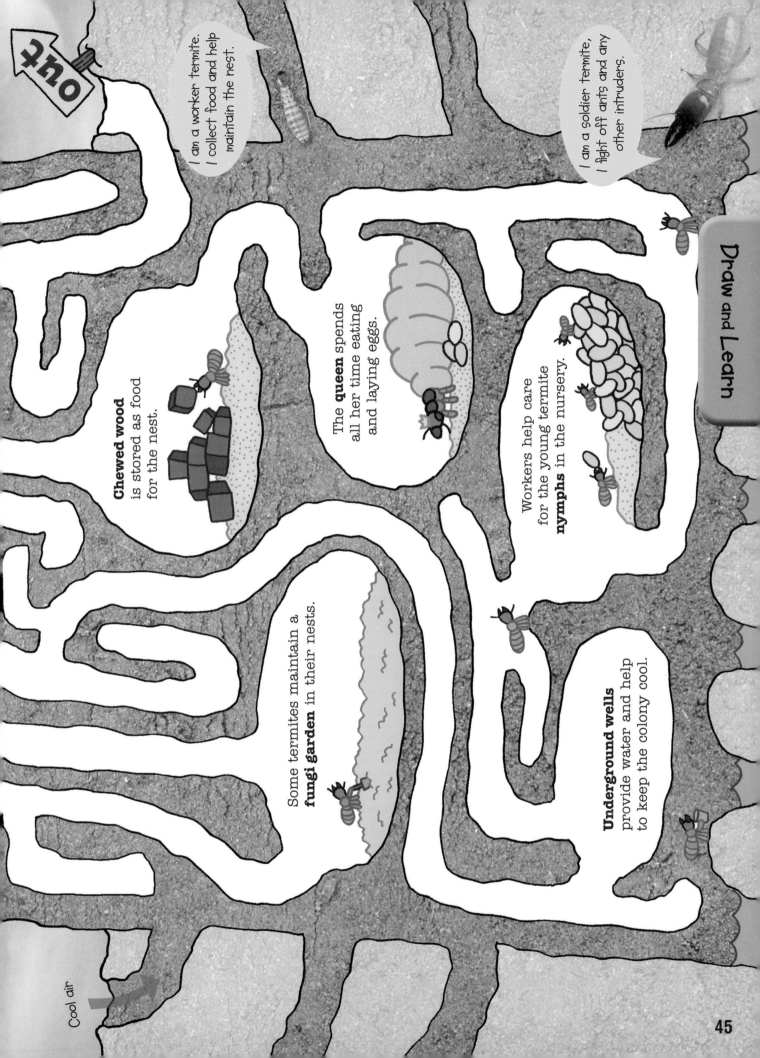

out

I am a worker termite. I collect food and help maintain the nest.

I am a soldier termite, I fight off ants and any other intruders.

Chewed wood is stored as food for the nest.

The **queen** spends all her time eating and laying eggs.

Workers help care for the young termite **nymphs** in the nursery.

Some termites maintain a **fungi garden** in their nests.

Underground wells provide water and help to keep the colony cool.

Cool air

Busy bees

Honeybees might just be our best friends in the insect world. Not only do they pollinate more flowers than any other creature on Earth, but they're also the reason we have delicious honey.

Honeybee quizzzz

Add the stickers with the answers.

What are the three types of honeybee that live in a hive?

How many honeybees can live in a single hive?

Why are honeycombs made up of hexagon shapes? (shapes with six sides)

How much honey can a single honeybee make in its lifetime.

How many queens are there in a hive?

Facts about...

Pollination

As bees fly from plant to plant they spread pollen, which **helps the plants to reproduce**. Other animals such as birds and beetles, also pollinate – but not as much as bees.

Colour in the flowers and add bee stickers.

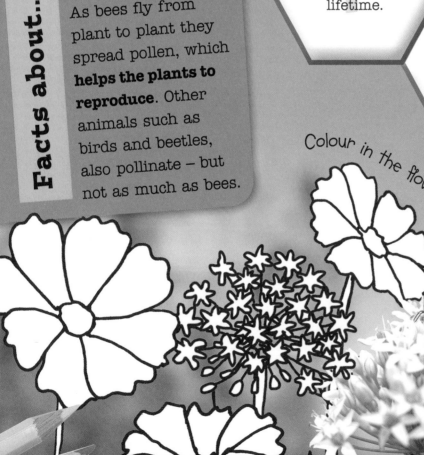

How do bees make honey?

Bees don't make honey for us on purpose, it's actually a product of **nectar**, which is collected from flowers and turned into food for the entire colony.

Fact Challenge

Facts about...

Colonies

Bee colonies are very organized, and bees work very hard. **Worker bees** tend to the queen, care for the young, collect and store nectar, and guard the hive.

STICK the honey in the honeycomb and jar, then read the bee facts.

4

3

2

1

Fill the jar with honey, starting at the bottom.

I gather nectar too, just not as much as honeybees do.

Bumble bee

Living in the rainforest

The world's rainforests are home to more life than anywhere else on Earth. This is the case for all animals and plants, but especially with arthropods.

Leaf-footed bugs have very unusual hind legs.

Fungus beetle

Caterpillar

COLOUR all the arthropods and the rest of the rainforest scene.

Dragonfly

Centipede

Jumping spider

Leaf cutter ants carry leaves back to their colonies.

Butterfly

Grasshopper

Stick insects look just like sticks. This can help them hide.

Amazing colours

Rainforests are a very diverse habitat, which means lots of different creatures live there – many of which are very colourful and unusual.

Facts about...

Full of life

All these species can be found in Manú National Park in Peru. Which is home to **thousands of species of arthropod**, as well as many mammals, fish, and reptiles.

Shield bug

Leaf katydids look just like leaves.

Scorpion

49

The unusual **WORLD** of bugs

Insects and other arthropods are the most diverse creatures on Earth. This diversity means that many of them have very bizarre and extreme abilities.

Page _____

Page _____

FIND

these pictures on pages 52–64 and write the page numbers in the boxes.

Page _____

Page _____

Page _____

Page _____

Survival experts

Cockroaches are one of the most resilient creatures on Earth, and can survive in many extreme conditions. How extreme? You be the judge.

ANSWER whether you think each cockroach fact is true or false.

1 Even if a cockroach's head is cut off, it can survive for up to a week.
TRUE FALSE

2 Cockroaches have existed for a billion years.
TRUE FALSE

3 Cockroaches can live without food for more than a month.
TRUE FALSE

4 Cockroaches are very slow-moving insects.
TRUE FALSE

5 Cockroaches have a deadly bite that injects their victim with a strong poison.
TRUE FALSE

That's impossible!

Many people believe that cockroaches can survive nuclear explosions. This isn't true, but cockroaches might be able to survive the **radiation** that follows them (which would kill most other living creatures).

WANTED

DEAD OR ALIVE

If you think the great white shark is the deadliest animal in the world, you're in for a surprise. Earth's most dangerous creature is actually the tiny mosquito!

Complete the picture

The world's deadliest animal

Why?

Mosquitos don't have a deadly poison or a powerful sting, but they can carry and spread diseases such as malaria and yellow fever, which kill around **725,000 people each year**.

How?

Female mosquitos suck human blood in order to gain the protein they need **to lay their eggs**. When they do this they can inject germs, which can spread and cause fatal diseases.

ANSWER

the true or false questions and complete the sticker jigsaw.

1 Only about 100 of the 3,500 species of mosquito suck blood.

TRUE ○ ○ FALSE

2 Mosquitos can grow to be the size of tennis balls.

TRUE ○ ○ FALSE

3 Mosquito saliva contains a painkiller so people can't feel their bites.

TRUE ○ ○ FALSE

buzzzzz **buzzzzzzz**

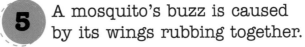

Actual size

Antenna

Proboscis

Wings

Many countries have wiped out the diseases spread by mosquitos, but it's still a big problem in poorer parts of the world.

4 Mosquito bites are very painful.

TRUE ○ ○ FALSE

5 A mosquito's buzz is caused by its wings rubbing together.

TRUE ○ ○ FALSE

6 Only female mosquitos suck human blood.

TRUE ○ ○ FALSE

Facts about...

Malaria

The most common disease spread by mosquitos is malaria. It causes a **strong fever** which is very dangerous and can be fatal if it isn't treated.

Butterfly
colours

Butterflies might be one of the prettiest types of insect, but their brightly coloured patterns aren't just for show. They also help butterflies to hide from, and even trick, predators.

Dark form
The female **eastern tiger swallowtail**, seen below, has two forms. One is bright yellow, the other is black.

Clever colours
Many, but not all, butterflies that are **orange and black** are poisonous, so predators often avoid any butterflies with that colouring.

Symmetry
The patterns and colours on butterfly wings aren't just beautiful – they're also very interesting. Each wing looks like the **reflection** of the other. This is known as symmetry.

Facts about...

COLOUR
each of the butterflies using the colour key at the bottom.

A clever disguise

When the peacock butterfly's wings are open it looks as if it has a **large pair of eyes** on its back. This can trick birds and other predators into thinking it's a much larger animal.

See if you can spot the "eyes" once the butterfly is coloured in.

I'm bright on top but when I close my wings it helps me to hide.

Colour each part as shown on the key.

Key

1
2
3
4
5
6
7

Weird and wonderful

STICK the arthropods in the correct places and read about each one.

Red-kneed tarantula

Type: Arachnid

Top size: Up to 18cm (7in) long

Life span: Up to 30 years

Fact: Sometimes kept as a pet. If a tarantula loses a leg a new one can grow back in its place.

> Queen fire ants can live for up to 6 years.

Stick insect

Type: Insect

Top size: Up to 30cm (12in) long

Life span: Up to 2 years

Fact: This insect looks just like a twig, and sometimes plays dead to help keep itself safe from predators.

Fire ant

Type: Insect

Top size: Up to 6mm (¼in) long

Life span: Up to 60 days

Fact: Fire ant colonies can contain more than 500,000 ants. Fire ants attack predators in large numbers in an organized way.

Tiger beetle

Type: Insect

Top size: Up to 4cm (1½in) long

Life span: Up to 6 weeks

Fact: It can move at speeds of up to 170 body lengths per second, which would be like a human running 350kph (217mph).

Decorator crab

Type: Crustacean

Top size: Up to 5cm (2in) long

Life span: Up to 10 years

Fact: Collects shells, seaweed, and other small animals, then attaches them to its body to help stay hidden.

Black widow spider

Type: Arachnid

Top size: Up to 4cm (1½in) long

Life span: Up to 3 years

Fact: The female black widow has a red hourglass pattern on its abdomen, and it's bite can deliver a deadly poison.

Firefly

Type: Insect

Top size: Up to 2.5cm (1in) long

Life span: Up to 1 month

Fact: Also known as a "lightning bug", a firefly is a type of beetle. It can emit a glowing light from special organs on its abdomen.

Almost all of Earth's animals are amazing in one way or another, but no creatures come in as many strange forms as arthropods.

The puss moth caterpillar's whip-like tail.

Armoured millipede

Type: Myriapod

Top size: Up to 20cm (8in) long

Life span: Up to 10 years

Fact: In addition to its armour, this millipede has a poison to protect itself from predators.

Some mayflies only live for a few minutes!

Mayfly

Type: Insect

Top size: Up to 2cm (¾in) long

Life span: Up to 2 days

Fact: An adult mayfly doesn't have a working mouth. It only lives long enough to reproduce, and doesn't need to eat.

Fact Challenge

Puss moth caterpillar

Type: Insect

Top size: Up to 7cm (2¾in) long

Life span: Up to 2 weeks (before becoming a puss moth)

Fact: It waves around the whip-like section at its rear in defence. It can also spray an acid at its enemies.

A swarm of locusts

COUNT how many locusts there are in the scene.

These grasshoppers may not look like much, but after going through a dramatic change, they gather together in a feeding frenzy and cause huge damage to crops.

Don't count this timid green one!

Facts about...

Sudden change
Locusts can change from **timid green grasshoppers** into eating machines — becoming stronger, darker, and quicker, as well as changing their behaviour.

We don't bite humans but we do like to eat their crops!

As locusts change they become organized, and eat any crops in sight.

Getting bigger

Like a lot of other insects, as locusts grow they **shed their exoskeletons** and emerge looking different. This process is known as ecdysis.

Old skin

The locust wriggles out of its old skin, becoming larger and darker.

Draw and Learn

Split personality

Locusts transform because of a chemical called **serotonin**. When food is in short supply and the hoppers gather in one place, their serotonin levels increase, which causes them to change.

TRUE OR FALSE?

Large swarms spread for miles, and can contain more than a billion locusts.

Yum! I'll eat everything in my path!

59

Silent hunters

The praying mantis is one of the deadliest hunters of the insect world. It blends into its environment to go unnoticed, and can rotate its head 180° to look for nearby prey.

Lying in wait

The praying mantis is an ambush hunter. It will hide in plain sight, staying motionless until its prey is nearby, then leap forward with lightning speed to snatch the victim.

Ahh!

Lunch

Spikes on its arms help it to grip prey.

Suddenly, the mantis springs forward and snatches its prey.

A mantis will stay perfectly still until its prey is in reach.

We have something rare in insects called "binocular vision" which helps us spot prey.

Let me gooooooo!

The mantis brings its prey close and bites off its head!

STICK
the stickers into the grid to complete the praying mantis puzzle.

Facts about...
Mantis
After mating, the female praying mantis sometimes **bite off** the male's head. Scientists believe they do this to get extra energy to produce eggs.

17 year Cicadas

Famous for having a very unusual life cycle, some cicadas spend up to 17 years underground – surfacing only to mate and live a very short adult life.

COLOUR

the rest of the pictures to finish the story of cicada life cycles.

Fully grown cicadas have hard black bodies and amazing red eyes.

Facts about...

Cicada songs

The sound of millions of cicadas all buzzing together creates a very distinct and unusual sound. It's actually the **loudest sound** in the insect world.

Some cicadas stay underground for 13 years instead.

For 17 years...

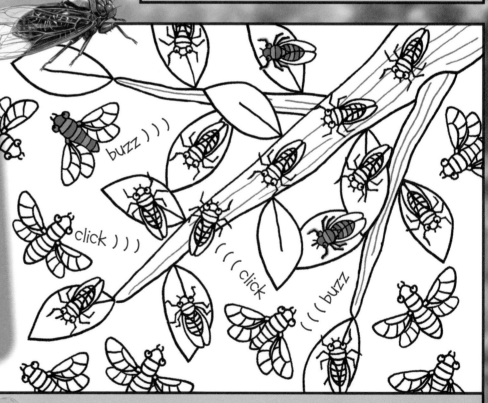

1 Young cicadas, also known as **nymphs**, can live underground for up to **17 years** feeding on the sap from tree roots.

buzz)))

click)))

((((click

(((((buzz

4 Slowly their wings expand and their bodies harden and **turn black**. The cicadas then begin to look for a mate. To attract each other, the males make a buzzing sound and the females flick their wings together to make a clicking sound.

...one warm evening

2 When the time is right, **millions of cicadas** crawl out of the ground during the night and climb into trees.

The next day

Empty skin

3 The cicadas shed their skins and crawl out with their adult bodies. At first they have shrivelled wings and **soft white bodies**.

5 After mating the male dies instantly. The female then lays **hundreds of eggs** into gaps in the tree and dies shortly after.

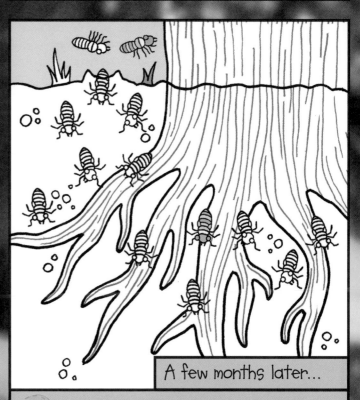

A few months later...

6 Eventually the cicadas hatch from the eggs and the young cicadas fall to the ground. They then burrow underground to **wait for 17 years** to repeat the cycle.

Design
your own bug

The arthropod world is full of wonderful and fascinating creatures, and new species are being discovered all the time. Can you make up one of your own?

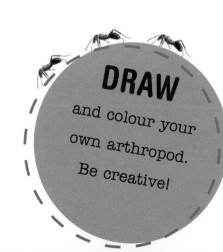

DRAW
and colour your own arthropod. Be creative!

Piece together the beetle on **page 3** with these.

These stickers are for **pages 4–5**.

Stick these **extras** anywhere.

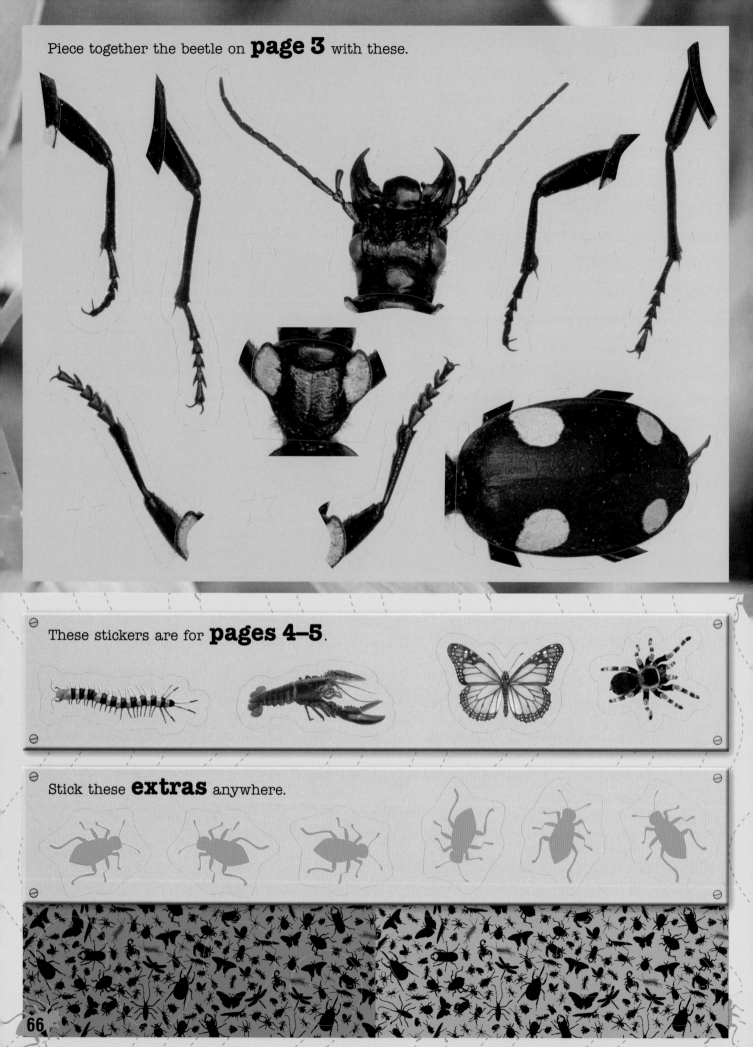

66

Fill the arthropod family tree on **pages 6–7** with these.

Insects

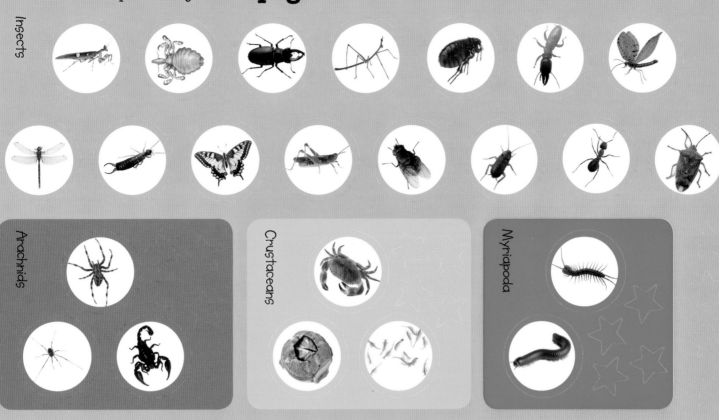

Arachnids

Crustaceans

Myriapoda

These stickers are all **extras**.

These butterflies and moths are for **pages 12–13**.

Stick these crustaceans on **pages 16–17**.

70

Use these **extra ones** anywhere you like!

These stickers are for the activity on **page 19**.

These baby bugs belong on **pages 20–21**.

Use these stickers on **pages 26–27**.

Use these for the puzzle on **page 29**.

Use these extra ones anywhere you like.

Fill the dinner plate on **pages 30–31** with these.

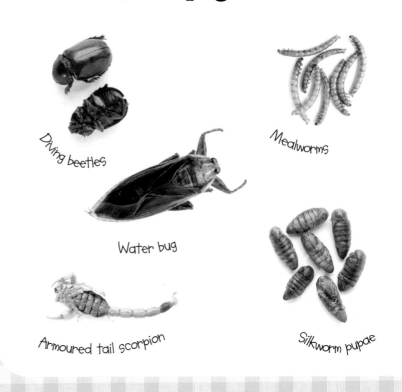

Diving beetles

Mealworms

Water bug

Armoured tail scorpion

Silkworm pupae

Add these flying bugs to **pages 32–33**.

Longwing butterfly

Oak eggar moth

Desert locust

Hover fly

Bumblebee

Hawk moth

Wasp

Lacewing

Green-eyed dragonfly

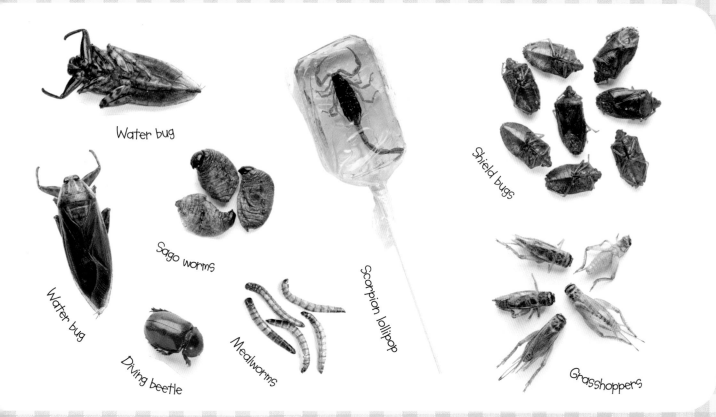

Water bug

Sago worms

Scorpion lollipop

Shield bugs

Water bug

Diving beetle

Mealworms

Grasshoppers

Gulf fritillary butterfly

Cockchafer beetle

Bumblebee

Lacewing

Peacock butterfly

Indian cicada

Cardinal beetle

Longwing butterfly

Cockchafer beetle

Black wasp

Lacewing

Stick these creatures and their memorable eyes on **page 35**.

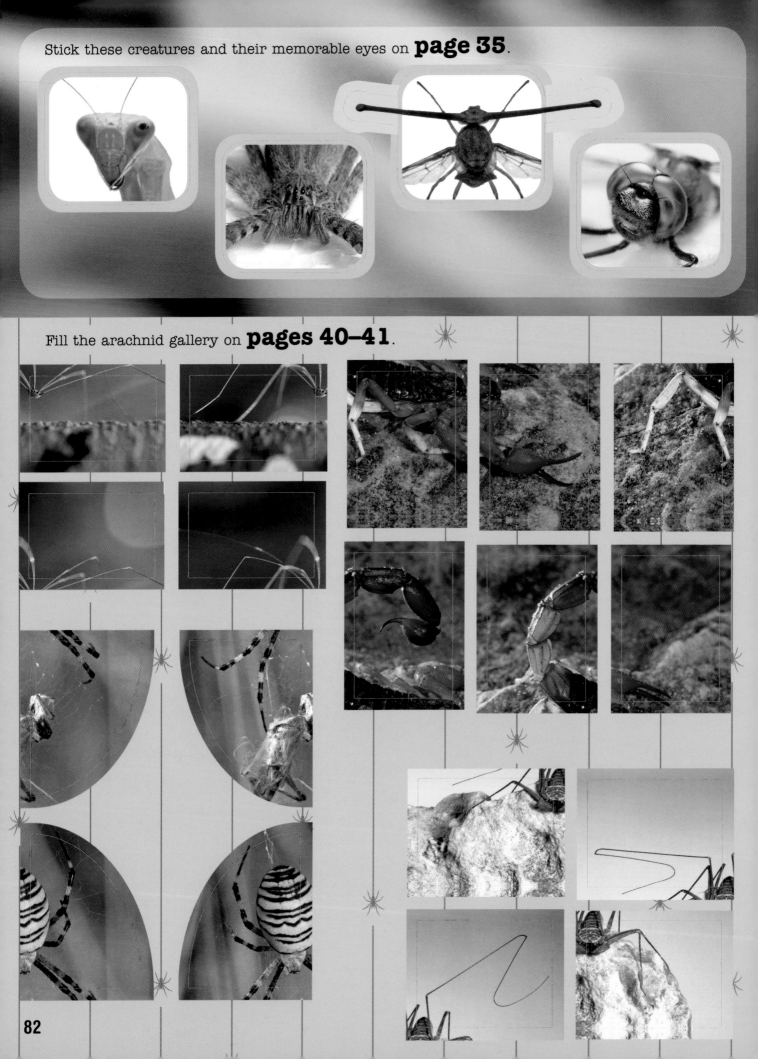

Fill the arachnid gallery on **pages 40–41**.

Stick the labels by the ant's body on **page 38**.

Eye   Claw   Leg   Mandible   Abdomen

Use these **extra ones** anywhere you like.

These little ones are **extras**.

Fill the box on **pages 42–43** with these beetles.

Use these **extra stickers** anywhere you like.

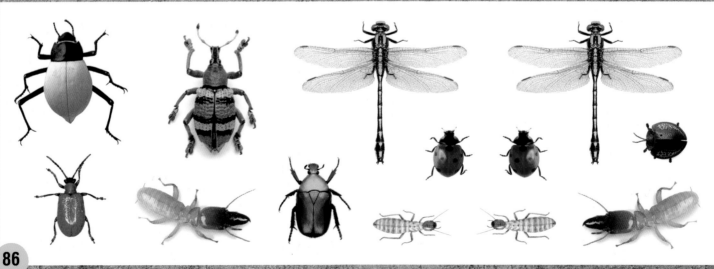

Hexagons are one of the strongest shapes for building, so the hives rarely collapse.

Honeybee hives can contain up to **80,000 bees**.

Each honeybee will produce about **1 teaspoon** of honey in its lifetime.

There is only one **queen** in a honeybee hive.

Hives **are made up** of a queen, thousands of workers, and a few hundred male drones.

3

The collected nectar mixes with **special enzymes** inside the bee's stomach, turning it into honey.

1

Bees fly around looking for **nectar**, which is a sweet liquid found in certain types of flowers.

4

The bees place the honey in a hexagonal shape and quickly **flap their wings** to drive off excess water.

2

When a bee finds nectar, it does a **special dance** to let other bees know there's more to collect.

Stick this deadly mosquito on **page 52**. The other stickers are extras.

Use these **extra stickers** anywhere you like!

Stick these butterflies wherever you want.

Add these stickers to **pages 56–57**.

Use these to complete the mantis puzzle on **page 61**.

Use these **extra ones** anywhere you like.

These are **extras** to use anywhere.

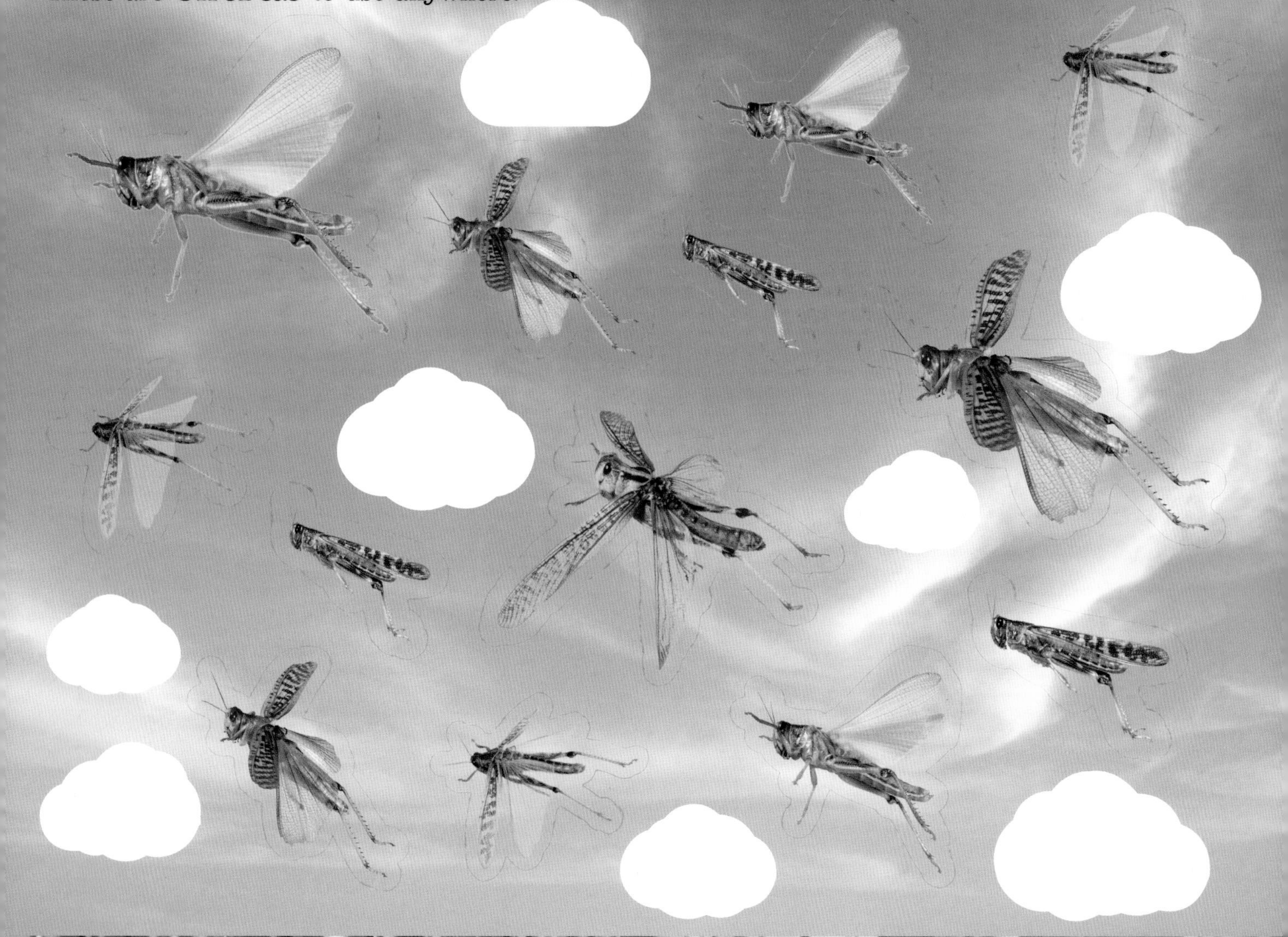

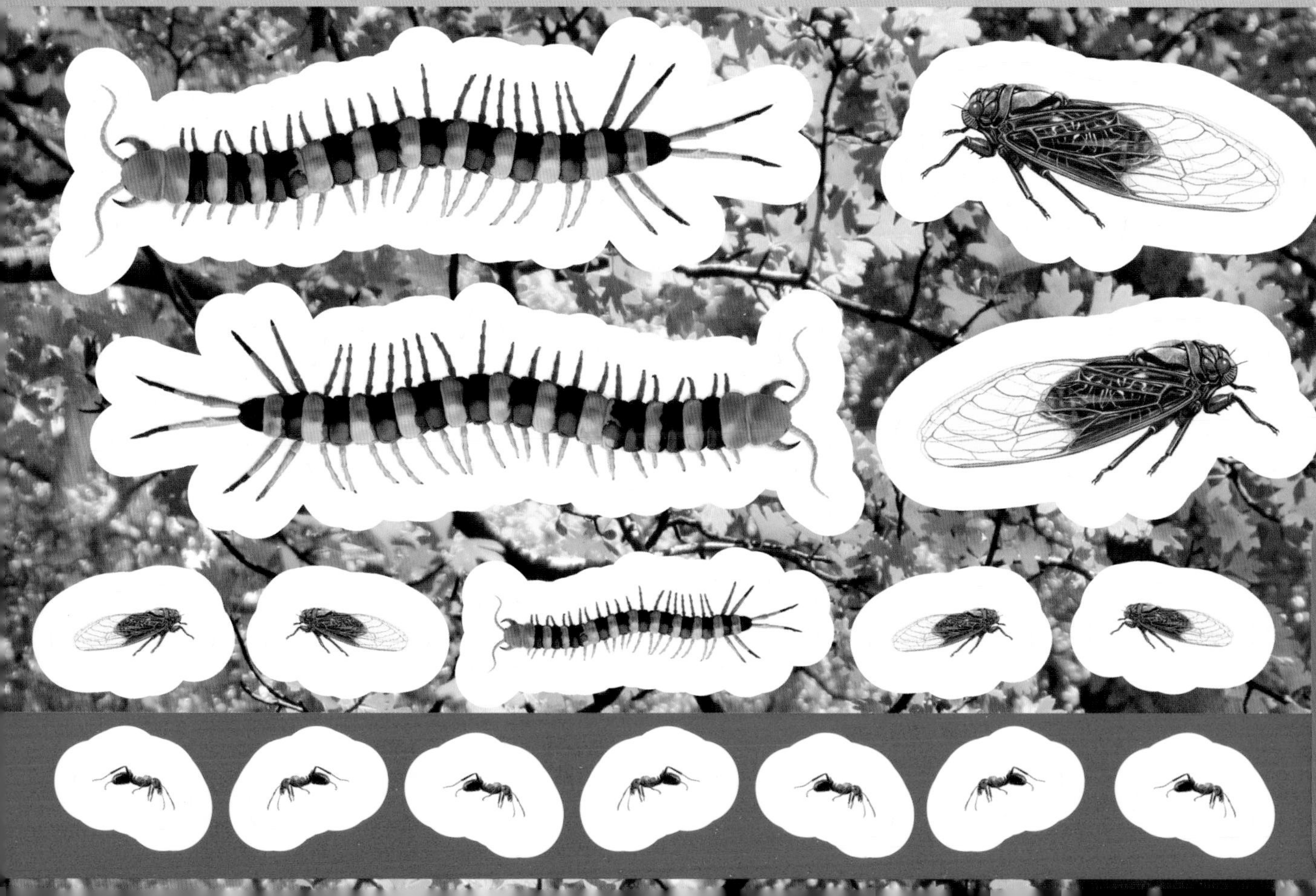